CLEOPATRA
THE QUEEN OF KINGS

Cleopatra rewards a loyal subject with a gold necklace.

Julius Caesar

Cleopatra is summoned to Tarsus by Antony.

A millefiori (thousands of flowers) glass drinking cup

Cleopatra's younger brother seizes power.

A coin decorated with a cornucopia (horn of plenty)

Craftsmen work on Cleopatra's mausoleum

CLEOPATRA
THE QUEEN OF KINGS

Written by
FIONA MACDONALD

Illustrated by
CHRIS MOLAN

DK

A Dorling Kindersley Book

LONDON, NEW YORK, MUNICH,
MELBOURNE and DELHI

Project Editor Sue Barraclough
Art Editor Catherine Goldsmith
Senior Editor Marie Greenwood
Senior Art Editor Carole Oliver
Publishing Manager Jayne Parsons
Managing Art Editor Jacquie Gulliver
DTP Designer Nomazwe Madonko
Picture Researcher Franziska Marking
Jacket Designer Dean Price
Production Kate Oliver, Jenny Jacoby
Consultant Dr Sally-Ann Ashton
Special photography Max Alexander, Alistair Duncan,
Christi Graham and Nick Nichols, Peter Hayam, John Heseltine,
Dave King, Stephen Oliver, Lawrence Pardes, Tony Souter

Additional illustrations by John James

Hardback edition first published in Great Britain in 1998
This edition published in Great Britain in 2003
by Dorling Kindersley Limited,
80 Strand, London, WC2R 0RL

2 4 6 8 10 9 7 5 3 1

Copyright © 1998, © 2003, Dorling Kindersley Ltd., London

A CIP catalogue record for this book is available
from the British Library.

ISBN 0 7513 3916 4

Reproduced by Colourscan, Singapore
Printed and bound by L.E.G.O., Italy

see our complete
catalogue at
www.dk.com

Contents

Cleopatra's Egypt

FOR OVER 3,000 YEARS, EGYPT WAS HOME TO A RICH and splendid civilization. But by 69 BC, when Cleopatra VII was born, Egypt's power was failing. The country was ruled by a dynasty (family) of pharaohs, all called Ptolemy, who had arrived from Macedonia in 323 BC. Egypt was also in danger of being taken over by its great rival, Rome. The first Ptolemies had ruled well, but their descendants, including Cleopatra's father, were weak and even foolish. Cleopatra faced an uncertain future. But she was to become a daring and courageous queen, and one of the most famous women who has ever lived.

Harold Oakley's watercolour of the Pharos is based on a reconstruction, made in the late 19th century.

Alexandria, Cleopatra's home, was a bustling port on the Mediterranean Sea. The early Ptolemies encouraged science, art, and trade and introduced many new ideas and inventions to Egypt.

The Pharos tower was the world's first lighthouse. Built around 280 BC, it was destroyed by an earthquake in the 14th century. Today it is remembered as one of the Seven Wonders of the Ancient World.

Harold Oakley

FAMILY AT WAR

FROM AN EARLY AGE, CLEOPATRA knew that her family was at war – with the people it ruled, and with itself. The people suffered under the cruelty of Cleopatra's father – Ptolemy XII – and they resented his alliance with Rome. In 58 BC, the citizens of Alexandria rioted, and chased Ptolemy out of Egypt. Ptolemy fled to Rome, and Cleopatra's older sister, Berenice, became queen. In 55 BC, Ptolemy returned to Egypt. Helped by Roman general Pompey he snatched back power from Berenice, and ruled as pharoah once more. Ptolemy then gave orders for Berenice to be executed.

Pompey the Great
Pompey (106–48 BC) was one of the most brilliant generals of his time. By helping Ptolemy XII he hoped to increase Roman power in Egypt.

CLEOPATRA VII
At 14 Cleopatra had seen her father flee for his life and family members killed. She must have wondered how long she would survive.

RIVALS FOR POWER
All Ptolemy XII's children hoped to rule, and this made them rivals. Cleopatra's older sister, Berenice IV, ruled from 58–55 BC. Her sister, Cleopatra Tryphaena, died mysteriously around this time – the rumour was that Berenice had murdered her.

PTOLEMY XII
Ptolemy XII was pharoah of Egypt during the years 80–58 BC and 55–51 BC. Ptolemy was disliked by his subjects because he collected heavy taxes and sent the money to Rome. Ptolemy hoped that if he made friends with the Roman leaders and paid the Romans enough money, they would not invade his land.

Ptolemy XIII   Ptolemy XIV

Berenice   Cleopatra Tryphaena   Arsinoe

CLEOPATRA'S BROTHERS
Cleopatra had two younger brothers, both called Ptolemy according to family custom. They were both to become rulers of Egypt – as Ptolemy XIII and Ptolemy XIV.

CLEOPATRA'S SISTERS
Ptolemy had four daughters. Cleopatra's sisters were called Berenice IV, Cleopatra Tryphaena VI, and Arsinoe IV. By 55 BC Cleopatra had only one sister still alive – the youngest, Arsinoe.

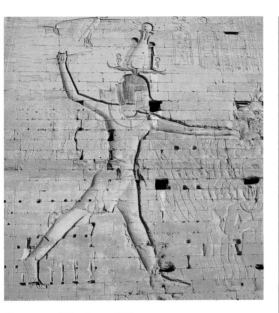

Portrait of Ptolemy XII
The Ptolemies paid to have their portraits carved in ancient Egyptian style, even though they were from Macedonia (northern Greece). They wanted to link themselves with the great pharoahs of Egypt's past. This carving, at the Temple of Horus at Edfu, shows Ptolemy XII conquering his enemies.

THE ROMAN EMPIRE
While the Ptolemies faced problems in Egypt, the Roman empire continued to expand. By 55 BC the Roman army had conquered land in northern and southern Europe, in north Africa and in the Middle East.

Symbols of power

CLEOPATRA'S FAMILY, the Ptolemies, introduced many changes to Egypt. One of the most important was the use of coins for trade. Before the Ptolemies, coins were almost unknown; Egyptian merchants bartered (exchanged) goods instead. Coins also carried a political message. Images on the Ptolemies' coins showed them as rich and powerful.

This beautiful portrait shows a Ptolemaic queen – Berenice II, sister and wife of Ptolemy III.

A cornucopia (horn overflowing with fruit and grain) – symbol of wealth and prosperity.

The Roman army was a formidable fighting machine. Many thousands of well-trained soldiers marched into battle to win new lands for Rome.

The coast around the Nile Delta was very flat, so the huge lighthouse helped ships find their way into Alexandria harbour.

Alexandria was a flourishing port on the Meditteranean. The rulers of Rome relied on Egypt to supply the people of its empire with grain and other foodstuffs.

Nile Delta

FRANCE

GREECE

Rome
ITALY

Actium

SPAIN

MEDITERRANEAN SEA

Alexandria
EGYPT

Between c. 200-55 BC the Roman empire expanded so rapidly that Rome often had to rely on "puppet" kings to run the countries for them.

THE SUN GOD'S DAUGHTER

CLEOPATRA WAS NOW PTOLEMY XII'S oldest surviving child. When he died she would become queen, as the wife of her younger brother, Ptolemy XIII. This was exciting, but also terrifying. Cleopatra remembered what had happened to her sisters, and feared that enemies might try to kill her too. But Cleopatra was clever. She made friends with powerful courtiers. She prepared herself for government by learning many languages including Egyptian (all the other members of her family only spoke Greek). She also used religion to support her claim to the throne. Cleopatra called herself the Sun-God's daughter, which was an ancient royal title.

Homes for the gods
Temples were built as homes for the gods. The priests made offerings of food, drink, and incense to the holy statues every day. The more important temples were wealthy, powerful organizations. They owned farms, orchards, libraries, and workshops, and employed many servants.

The sacred bull of Buchis
Egyptians believed that the sacred bulls, in a temple at Buchis, were the sun-god Amun-Re in animal form. Soon after she became queen, Cleopatra travelled down the Nile with a newly chosen Buchis bull. To the Egyptian people, the bulls were gods, and by taking part in the ceremony, Cleopatra was showing the people that she respected their gods.

Inner shrine
Only members of the royal family or senior priests and priestesses could enter the dark inner shrine of each temple, where the statue of the god or goddess stood.

MAKING MUSIC
Musicians, singers, and dancers performed holy music while Cleopatra made offerings of food and flowers.

Gods and goddesses

LIKE ALL THE Ptolemies and their queens before her, Cleopatra said prayers and made offerings to many of the gods and goddesses of ancient Egypt. Traditionally, Isis and Hathor protected Egyptian queens from harm.

Amun Re, lord of the Sun, was the mightiest god of all.

Isis was goddess of magic and healing.

Hathor was goddess of motherhood, music, and love.

" The Queen, the Lady of the Two Lands, the father-loving goddess, rowed the Bull in the barge of Amon to Hermonthis. **"**

Translated from a stele (stone slab) at Hermonthis (now called Amant).

POWERFUL FRIENDS

Cleopatra needed the support of priests who belonged to rich, powerful families. All priests received a share of offerings made to the gods, and of the profits from temple lands. Priests spent time away from their temples and many served as senior officials at court. So Cleopatra gave generous gifts to the most important temples, to encourage their priests to help her stay in power.

INSIDE THE TEMPLE
To reach the inner shrine, worshippers walked in a solemn procession through the great hypostyle hall at the front of the temple, with its massive carved and painted columns.

MAGNIFICENT HEADDRESS
Like other Ptolemaic queens, Cleopatra wore a tall headdress of gold plumes (symbol of the god Amun), with a sun-disk and a pair of horns (symbols of the goddesses Hathor and Isis).

Sweet-smelling incense was burned as an offering to the gods.

Teenage Queen

An Egyptian throne – a symbol of royal power.

ANCIENT RECORDS INDICATE THAT CLEOPATRA RULED with her father for a short time. And after his death in 51 BC, 18-year-old Cleopatra was determined to hold onto power. In keeping with the traditions of the time, she married her 12-year-old brother, Ptolemy XIII. (Like all the Ptolemies before her, she did not want to marry outside the royal family, because that might weaken its power.) In law, Ptolemy now had the right to rule, but his sister said that he was too young. Cleopatra wanted to rule – alone. However, Cleopatra knew that many nobles and royal officials supported her brother's right to rule. And General Pompey, her dead father's powerful ally, had plans to govern Egypt for Rome. The young Cleopatra knew she would need to use all her charm and intelligence to remain queen.

> " If Cleopatra's nose had been shorter, the whole face of the world would have been changed. "
>
> Blaise Pascal (French philosopher), commenting on Cleopatra's legendary beauty. From his *Pensées* (Thoughts) c.1670.

A carved relief in traditional Egyptian style at the Temple of Hathor at Dendera.

ROYAL PORTRAIT
Cleopatra clearly
had a powerful
and fascinating
personality, even
when young.
Throughout history,
she has always been
portrayed as beautiful,
as in this marble head.
However, nobody knows for
sure what she actually looked like.

Water-wheel
This beautiful wall-painting shows an ox harnessed to a *sakkiyeh* (a wooden water-wheel). As the ox walked round, the wheel turned, lifting water from the Nile to the fields. Oxen still pull water-wheels in Egypt today.

> ❝For by nature the land produces more fruit than do other lands, and still more when watered...❞
>
> Strabo, from *Geography*, c. 100 BC

FACT file

• The Nile is the world's longest river. It runs for 6,690 km (4,160 miles) from the highlands of Central Africa to the Mediterranean Sea.

• Today, the Nile is dammed at Aswan, but in Cleopatra's time it flooded in June because of rainwater it carried from the highlands. The land beside the river remained underwater until August or September.

• After the floods, the land was covered in thick, fertile mud. It was dry enough to plough by November, the start of the Egyptian farmers' year.

LIFE IN CLEOPATRA'S EGYPT

CLEOPATRA AND HER FAMILY LIVED IN Alexandria, Egypt's splendid capital city. The city had been founded by Alexander the Great in 331 BC, and it had grown and prospered over 300 years of rule by the Ptolemies. Alexandria was one of the most important ports in the ancient world, and it was home to an exciting multicultural civilization, which blended Greek, Egyptian, and Middle Eastern ideas and beliefs. But to most ordinary Egyptians, Alexandria seemed strange and foreign – just like the Ptolemies themselves. In the first two years of Cleopatra's reign the Nile failed to flood. There were crop failures and famines, and many ordinary people starved. As ruler of Egypt, Cleopatra needed to help the people and win their support – but she also needed to please the sophisticated citizens of Alexandria.

TRAVELLING BY BOAT
This wooden model of a boat was found in a tomb. Egyptians would have sailed up and down the Nile to take crops to market, to visit temples, and to trade.

UNDER SAIL
Sailing along the river was much quicker and safer than travelling overland. People and goods could be transported easily from place to place.

Alexandria was a busy port with boats coming and going from all over the Meditteranean.

MEDITERRANEAN SEA

● Alexandria

NILE DELTA

The main crops were wheat and barley, which were used to make bread and beer - the Egyptians' staple (basic) foods.

The Fayum

Farmers dug networks of ditches to bring water to their land. These divided the land into small plots.

Simple papyrus reed boats were used for short trips on the river.

RED SEA

River Nile

Sail boats followed important trade routes through the Red Sea to countries in Africa and the Middle East.

Pots were shaped by hand, or on a potter's wheel. Potters also made clay tiles, painted with beautiful flower patterns.

● Dendera

● Hermonthis

Baskets were woven from papyrus or date-palm fibres. They were used to store and transport food.

Edfu ●

Precious stones and metals such as turquoise and gold, were mined all over Egypt.

Berenice ●

The Ptolemies built a new trading post called Berenice, on the shores of the Red Sea.

BESIDE THE NILE

Most Egyptian families lived in country towns and villages beside the swirling waters of the River Nile. They worked as farmers, builders, traders, and craftworkers, as their ancestors had done for thousands of years.

The Fayum

The Fayum is a large area of low-lying land in the desert of northern Egypt, surrounding a fresh-water lake. The soil is fertile, and the lake provides water for growing crops. Under the rule of the Ptolemies many Greek settlers moved there, and it was a busy and prosperous area.

Irrigation – watering the land

Egyptian farmers also used a *shaduf* (a bucket fixed to a long wooden arm) to lift water from the river to irrigate their land. The Ptolemies introduced a machine for lifting water – called an Archimedian Screw – from Greece to Egypt.

More wine!

BEFORE THE RULE of the Ptolemies wine was rare and expensive, and most Egyptians drank beer. The Greeks preferred wine so they brought new wine-making skills to Egypt.

This wall-painting shows farm workers harvesting and treading grapes.

INTO EXILE

FOR THE FIRST TWO YEARS OF HER REIGN Cleopatra managed to keep control of Egypt, but she had many enemies. One of the most powerful was Pothinus, her brother Ptolemy's chief advisor. He did not like the way Cleopatra made many important government decisions without consulting him. Also Ptolemy XIII was nearly 16 years old, and was demanding his share of power. In 48 BC, Cleopatra discovered that Ptolemy and Pothinus were plotting to send soldiers to kidnap her, and guessed that they planned to kill her. Cleopatra knew that she must leave Egypt. She set sail for Syria. There, Cleopatra hoped to recruit an army, to help her win back her throne from her brother who had now seized the throne.

Ptolemy's advisors
Young Ptolemy XIII relied heavily on advice given by top official Pothinus and leaders of rival groups of nobles at the Egyptian royal court.

Ruling alone
Cleopatra angered Ptolemy XIII and his supporters with displays of her own power, like this bronze coin, struck early in her reign. It carries her portrait and does not show her brother and co-ruler.

SEEKING SUPPORT
Cleopatra chose to go to Syria because the Ptolemies had once ruled there. The king of Syria was also an enemy of Rome. Like Cleopatra, he feared that his own country would be taken over by the mighty Roman empire.

SISTERS TOGETHER
Cleopatra took her only surviving sister, Arsinoe, into exile with her. This was partly to protect her from Ptolemy and Pothinus, but more importantly to stop Arsinoe trying to seize power.

DANGEROUS JOURNEY
It was a dangerous journey to Syria. The Mediterranean Sea was often troubled by violent squalls, and shipwrecks were common.

BATTLE FOR POWER

Julius Caesar and Pompey had once been close comrades, but in 48 BC they became rivals for supreme power in Rome. Their clash led to fighting between rival Roman armies, ending with the Battle of Pharsalus at which Julius Caesar was victorious.

Julius Caesar

Pharsalus

Cleopatra sailed to Syria, seeking support.

SYRIA

Cleopatra travelled back overland to Egypt.

MEDITERRANEAN SEA

Cleopatra's ship

After the Battle of Pharsalus, Pompey sailed directly to Egypt. Caesar was never far behind him.

Alexandria

EGYPT

Pompey

A TREACHEROUS ACT

While Cleopatra sought help in Syria, her guardian Pompey hurried to Egypt where he hoped that Ptolemy and Cleopatra would offer him money and soldiers. But Ptolemy's supporters murdered Pompey as soon as he landed in Alexandria.

KEEPING WATCH
Lookouts kept watch for pirates who raided ships with valuable cargo.

> *It was a delight to hear the sound of her voice. As if her voice was an instrument of many strings, she could pass from one language to another ... and she seldom needed an interpreter.*
>
> Plutarch, from his
> *Life of Mark Antony*, c. AD 75

CLEVER AND CHARMING

CAESAR ARRIVED IN EGYPT IN 48 BC, just four days after Pompey was killed. When Caesar landed at Alexandria, Ptolemy XIII's supporters offered him Pompey's head as a gift. Caesar was horrified by this brutal murder. However, he wanted to keep the peace – he had come to Egypt to collect a huge sum of money that he claimed Cleopatra's father had owed him. So he ordered Cleopatra and Ptolemy to meet with him to discuss a peace treaty. Cleopatra did not trust her brother and knew that there was a real danger that she would be killed if she came face to face with any of his advisors. She knew that she needed Caesar's protection.

One night Cleopatra had herself smuggled into Caesar's room – she was about to use all her charm and intelligence to win his support.

UNDERCOVER
Some stories say that Cleopatra was hidden in a carpet and some inside a roll of bedding.

Courage and loyalty
A merchant called Apollodorus was persuaded by Cleopatra to risk his life to smuggle her into the heavily-guarded palace.

HIDDEN CHARMS
Caesar was astonished when the carpet was unrolled to reveal Cleopatra herself.

A GIFT FOR CAESAR
Rulers like Cleopatra often sent rich gifts to powerful people. So Caesar would not have been surprised when Cleopatra's servant brought him a beautiful carpet. Cleopatra quickly gained Caesar's support but she still had enemies in Alexandria. Caesar, who had arrived with only a small army of men, was happy to find an ally in such a hostile city.

Caesar's barber

Pothinus sent a message to Achillas outside the city, outlining his plan to murder Caesar.

A servant would have carried the message out of the palace.

PLOT AGAINST CAESAR

When Pothinus, Ptolemy's chief advisor, found out that Cleopatra had won Caesar's support, he plotted against him. Caesar's barber heard Pothinus's plans, and Pothinus was executed. Meanwhile Arsinoe escaped from the city to join forces with General Achillas and the Egyptian army against Caesar.

JULIUS CAESAR
Impressed by Cleopatra's courage and daring, Caesar was soon bewitched by her.

City of learning
Cleopatra used her knowledge and intelligence to stay in power. The Ptolemies helped to make Alexandria into a great centre of learning. In Cleopatra's time the library was the greatest in the world.

Hieroglyphs

Demotic

Greek

The Rosetta Stone
Texts of the three languages used in Egypt in Cleopatra's time can be seen on the Rosetta Stone: hieroglyphs (used for royal decrees and religious texts); demotic (a written, simplified form of hieroglyphs); and Greek (Cleopatra's mother tongue). Cleopatra was famous for her knowledge of these languages and many others.

The Rosetta Stone is a slab of basalt rock found near Rosetta in the Nile delta.

PTOLEMY'S FURY

When Ptolemy XIII heard that Cleopatra was with Caesar, he ran out of the palace and threw down his crown in a terrible rage. The palace was now under siege by the Egyptian army. In the hope of appeasing them, Caesar allowed Ptolemy to leave the city and join his sister Arsinoe and General Achillas. Days after the war in Alexandria ended, Ptolemy's body was found in the harbour.

Metal mirror
Mirror-glass had not been invented in Cleopatra's time, so mirrors were made of highly-polished metals. The handle of this mirror is shaped like a servant girl wearing a lotus-flower headdress.

Pretty pottery
Make-up was kept in decorated pottery containers like this. The matching stick was used to put on the make-up.

Malachite made green eye paint

Galena made black eye paint

Iron oxide, made ochre for lips and cheeks

Natural colours
Like earlier queens of Egypt, Cleopatra used make-up made from plants and minerals. Malachite (copper ore), galena (lead ore), and iron oxide were ground up and mixed with water to make colourings for eyes, lips, and cheeks.

Fragrances and flowers
The Egyptians valued the sacred lotus flower for its delicate perfume. They also made perfumes with oils made from fragrant woods like cedar, and from cinnamon, honey, myrrh, and henna.

ROYAL BEAUTY

CLEOPATRA KNEW THAT LOOKING good was important. An impressive appearance helped her to get her own way – with Caesar, and with the Egyptian people too. She chose what she wore for each occasion with care. It is thought that for official public duties, Cleopatra wore Egyptian costume – a long, pleated linen shift decorated with beads and embroidery. In the privacy of her palace, Cleopatra probably preferred Greek-style robes of soft linen or smooth silk. Whatever the occasion, Cleopatra knew that she must appear impressive, powerful, and in control.

KEEPING CLEAN
All Egyptians liked to feel clean and fresh. Wealthy Egyptians, like Cleopatra, would have had baths, while ordinary people washed in the River Nile.

HELPING HANDS
After bathing, Cleopatra's servants wrapped her in soft linen towels, and massaged her skin with fragrant oils.

Sweet-smelling lotus (water-lily) flowers were symbols of rebirth and new life after death.

LOOKING LIKE A QUEEN

With her traditional Egyptian gown, Cleopatra wore a heavy wig. She also wore thick make-up, Egyptian style. Her eyelids were coloured, her eyes were outlined, and her cheeks were rouged.

Ochre (red earth) or plant and seaweed extracts were painted on to tint lips.

Cleopatra wore soft leather sandals with metal trimmings.

SACRED CREATURES
Cats were sacred. A Roman was stoned to death in Alexandria for accidentally killing a cat.

Images of Cleopatra

WE DO NOT know what Cleopatra looked like – all the portraits that have survived look very different. The features and hairstyle of this Roman head match her coin portraits, but Cleopatra would always have worn a diadem (crown). Egyptian portraits show Cleopatra as a goddess, and were not intended to be life-like.

Roman head

Traditional Egyptian carving

FINISHING TOUCHES

Cleopatra wore beautiful jewellery, elaborate make-up, and rich perfume. Sometimes, her nails and the palms of her hands were decorated with patterns in henna.

ROYAL SYMBOL
The cobra represented the goddess Wadjet who was believed to protect kings and queens.

> **"Her beauty was not so striking that it stunned the onlooker, but she made an inescapable impression on people around her ... the intelligence of all that she said and did, was bewitching."**
>
> Plutarch, from his
> *Life of Mark Antony,*
> c. AD 75

A Powerful Protector

JULIUS CAESAR
Caesar was a brilliant army commander and ambitious ruler of Rome.

F OR THE FIRST TIME IN YEARS, CLEOPATRA felt secure. Her enemy Ptolemy XIII and his advisors were dead, and Caesar promised to protect her and her new husband – her surviving brother, 11-year-old Ptolemy XIV. With Caesar, she sailed down the Nile, to meet her subjects and impress them with her power. Rumours said that Cleopatra was pregnant with Caesar's child. When Caesar returned to Rome, he left 15,000 men to guard her.

The temple walls were decorated with carved reliefs. Huge portraits of Cleopatra and her son Caesarion (Caesar's child) were later carved here.

> **❝** The eldest of Ptolemy's sons being dead, Caesar settled the kingdom upon the youngest, in conjunction with Cleopatra, the elder of the two sisters, who had always continued under his protection and guardianship. **❞**
>
> Written by one of Julius Caesar's officers, from The Alexandrian War, 47 BC

The temple of Hathor, Dendera. Cleopatra may have visited the temple on her Nile cruise with Caesar to make offerings to the goddess Hathor.

TO CAESAR'S ROME

AFTER TAKING CONTROL IN EGYPT, Caesar returned to Rome in 46 BC where he was welcomed as a hero. Cleopatra soon hurried to join him. She claimed that she was negotiating a peace treaty between Egypt and Rome, but she also wanted to make sure of Caesar's protection. Cleopatra brought her son Caesarion and teenage pharoah Ptolemy XIV with her. She did not want her brother or his advisors to try to seize power in Egypt while she was away. Many Romans were shocked by the relationship between Caesar and Cleopatra. They were afraid that Caesar would name Caesarion as his heir – that Cleopatra's son would become ruler of Rome.

Arriving in Rome
This scene, from a Hollywood film called *Cleopatra* made in 1963, shows Cleopatra (played by Elizabeth Taylor) arriving in Rome with her son Caesarion.

ARSINOE IN CHAINS
Arsinoe was marched through the streets in chains as part of a huge parade to celebrate Caesar's victories in Gaul (France), Egypt, north-west Africa, and Turkey.

ANGRY CROWD
The Roman people thought it was wrong to humiliate Arsinoe this way and the guards had to use their spears to keep the angry crowd back.

CAESAR'S TRIUMPH

Caesar celebrated his victories by parading his captives through the streets of Rome. Cleopatra's sister, Arsinoe, who had led the Egyptian army against Caesar, was dragged through the streets bareheaded and in chains. It was a disgrace for a woman to appear in public this way – it was the custom for Roman women to wear a long cloak and veil outside their homes. However, Arsinoe was lucky, unlike other captives, she was not killed. Caesar feared that the Romans might riot if they saw a princess publicly executed.

TRIUMPH
The victory procession, or "triumph", was traditionally awarded to Roman heroes as a sign of honour and respect.

Temples and tributes

TO GIVE THANKS for his victory at the battle of Pharsalus, Julius Caesar built a new temple in Rome dedicated to Venus Genetrix (Venus the "Great Mother"). Caesar also paid for a beautiful statue of Cleopatra to be put on display in the temple – it showed her as a mother holding Caesarion in her arms.

A queen in Rome
Cleopatra stayed in one of Caesar's splendid villas in Rome. She held court there, inviting leading Romans to visit her and offering them rich gifts. She hoped to win their friendship and support.

Roman forum
This picture shows the ruins of the Roman forum (market square and meeting place) where Caesar built his temple to Venus Genetrix.

The goddess of love
Julius Caesar's family claimed descent from Venus. So it was a great honour for Cleopatra to have her statue in the temple.

VENUS.

THE DEATH OF CAESAR
As a reward for his victories, the Senate made Caesar dictator (sole ruler) for the next ten years in 46 BC. Two years later, he was made dictator for life. But some Romans feared that Caesar was becoming too powerful, and that he wanted to be king. About sixty conspirators decided he must be killed.

Julius Caesar was stabbed to death after a Senate meeting in 44 BC.

The plot to murder Caesar was led by Brutus and Cassius.

TROUBLES AT HOME

AFTER CAESAR WAS MURDERED in 44 BC, the shocking news spread like wildfire round the Roman world. Cleopatra – who was in Rome when the murder happened – lost no time in hurrying back to Egypt. Now that Caesar, her protector, was dead, her kingdom was once more in danger. Many hostile countries saw Egypt as a rich prize, and hoped to conquer it. Cleopatra kept her son Caesarion close by her side, because she feared that he might be murdered by Caesar's enemies. Ptolemy XIV disappeared mysteriously, and people said that Cleopatra had poisoned her brother, so that she could rule Egypt with her young son.

Power struggle
Life back in Egypt was not easy for Cleopatra. She tried to win support from Alexandrian nobles by offering them rich rewards. She appeared in a "window of audience" in the royal palace and threw gifts to the crowd. But many people still saw her as a traitor, because of her friendship with Caesar and her long visit to Rome.

Only some of Cleopatra's subjects were pleased to see her. The palace guards kept hostile crowds as far back as possible.

Cleopatra threw rewards down to her supporters waiting below.

Rich rewards

TRADITIONALLY, PHAROAHS AND queens of Egypt rewarded loyal service with rich gifts of necklaces made from gold. Like earlier royal rulers, the Ptolemy dynasty had a huge store of gold, jewels, and other treasures, which had been given to past pharoahs as tribute from conquered peoples, or paid as taxes.

Collar of honour
This necklace is called a collar of honour, and is made from rows of gold rings. Thousands of years ago it was given to an ancient Egyptian noble as a reward.

Guests lounged on couches, in typical Greek and Roman style. They would lean on their left arm, and eat with their right hand.

DRINKING AND DANCING
The city of Alexandria was a sophisticated and luxurious city. And evenings spent drinking wine and dancing had always been popular in the palaces of the Ptolemies.

Musicians, acrobats, and dancers entertained guests at Cleopatra's feasts.

Like all the Ptolemies, Cleopatra spared no expense to provide amusements and entertainments for her guests.

Guests lounged on their couches, eating from plates of food carried in by an army of servants.

Tables were set with gold and jewelled cups and plates. The couches were covered in the finest fabrics, often woven with gold and silver threads.

Extravagant stories
Stories abound about Cleopatra's extravagance. This 18th-century painting was inspired by the story that tells how Cleopatra dissolved a priceless pearl in wine and drank it. In fact, pearls are not harmed by wine.

Drinking cup
Alexandria was famous for producing beautifully decorated glassware, such as this pretty drinking cup.

Roman wedding
This carving shows a Roman wedding ceremony. Late in 40 BC, Antony's wife Fulvia died. Antony made a peace treaty with Octavian, and as a sign of friendship he married Octavian's sister, Octavia.

QUEEN OF KINGS

> **Cleopatrae Reginae Regvm Filorvm Regvm**
> To Cleopatra, Queen of Kings and her sons who are Kings "
>
> Latin inscription from official coins made on Antony's orders, 34 BC

CLEOPATRA CONTINUED TO RULE EGYPT, but Antony did not return for nearly four years. When he sailed back in 36 BC after a disastrous defeat in Parthia, Cleopatra welcomed him. She needed a strong ally to help her keep Egypt independent. Antony was bold and ambitious, and he had huge armies of loyal soldiers who were ready to fight for him. Antony planned to set up an empire in North Africa and the Middle East to challenge his rivals in Rome, and Cleopatra supported his plans because they would increase her own power. In 35 BC Cleopatra and Antony had a third child, a son whom they named Ptolemy Philadelphus. Early in 34 BC, Antony invaded Armenia and returned to Alexandria in triumph. In a magnificent ceremony Cleopatra was crowned "Queen of Kings", and all her children were given special royal titles.

A fleet of warships
Cleopatra needed warships to defend Egypt and keep control of the Middle Eastern lands that she and Antony claimed as part of their empire. Skilled Egyptian shipbuilders used timber from Middle Eastern lands, especially Syria, to construct a mighty fleet.

ROYAL TITLES
Cleopatra and Antony gave royal titles to their young children – they were named as rulers of the Middle Eastern lands that Antony controlled. It was a sign of their alliance and ambition.

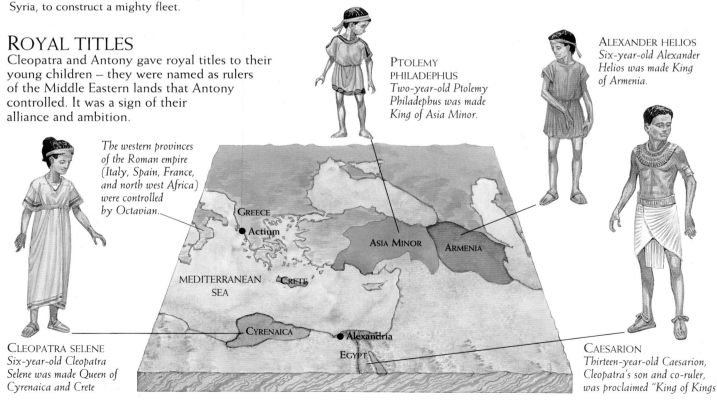

The western provinces of the Roman empire (Italy, Spain, France, and north west Africa) were controlled by Octavian.

GREECE
Actium
ASIA MINOR
ARMENIA
MEDITERRANEAN SEA
CRETE
CYRENAICA
Alexandria
EGYPT

PTOLEMY PHILADEPHUS
Two-year-old Ptolemy Philadephus was made King of Asia Minor.

ALEXANDER HELIOS
Six-year-old Alexander Helios was made King of Armenia.

CLEOPATRA SELENE
Six-year-old Cleopatra Selene was made Queen of Cyrenaica and Crete

CAESARION
Thirteen-year-old Caesarion, Cleopatra's son and co-ruler, was proclaimed "King of Kings'

ROYAL CROWN
As Queen of Kings, Cleopatra wore a crown with three snakes' heads. To the ancient Egyptians, the cobra was a sign of royal power.

PRECIOUS PEARLS
Pearls from the Indian Ocean were rare and valuable.

An ankh is an Egyptian symbol of life.

A cornucopia (horn of plenty), a Greek symbol of prosperity.

GREAT AMBITIONS

With Antony to help her, Cleopatra hoped to make Egypt the rich, civilized, and successful empire it had been when the first Ptolemies ruled, almost 300 years before. Cleopatra planned to reclaim the lands that the Ptolemies had once controlled outside Egypt. Many of these including Syria, Lebanon, Phoenicia, and parts of Asia Minor were given to her by Antony.

Royal reminder
In 34 BC Antony had silver coins made which showed Cleopatra's portrait and the inscription "Queen of Kings" on one side, and Antony's portrait on the other. It was a reminder of Cleopatra's royal power and a sign of their joint ambition.

Traitor!
When Octavian heard about Antony and Cleopatra's ambitious plans, he made powerful speeches in the Roman senate, declaring Antony as a traitor who no longer deserved the support of any Roman senator, citizen, or soldier.

A Roman senator

War with Rome

TOP ROMAN POLITICIANS, LED BY CAESAR'S nephew Octavian, were shocked by reports of Antony and Cleopatra's bid to set up an empire of their own. They were also angry that Antony had divorced his Roman wife. Late in 32 BC Octavian led a procession to Rome's temple of Bellona, goddess of war. Hurling a blood-tipped spear through the air, he declared war against Cleopatra – and all Egypt. Octavian knew that Antony still had supporters in Rome. But he felt sure the Romans would unite to fight against Egypt's ambitious queen.

This painting of the Battle of Actium (in the style of Eugen Schoen) is from *Panorama of World History*, by M. Reymond.

Battle-axe

Short sword

Dagger

A variety of weapons were used at this time. While Egyptian soldiers fought with battle-axes and hatchets, Roman soldiers used three main weapons — a long sword, for slashing; a short sword, for stabbing, and a dagger, for close combat.

"Antony bore witness to Caesarion that he was sprung from Caesar... gave enormous presents to his children by the Egyptian queen... and ordered that his body be buried by her side."

Dio Cassius, from his *Roman History*, c. AD 155

THE BATTLE OF ACTIUM

AS CLEOPATRA'S FRIEND AND OCTAVIAN'S RIVAL, Antony joined in the war against Rome. Antony also did not want to lose control of his lands in the east of the Roman empire, which included Greece. Fearing an attack by Rome, Antony and Cleopatra sailed to Greece with a huge fleet of warships. In spring 31 BC the Roman forces arrived, and for several months Octavian's fleet patrolled the Greek coast, fighting Antony's soldiers, capturing his forts and sinking his ships. Worst of all, they trapped Antony and Cleopatra's fleet in the Gulf of Ambracia. The land around the gulf was marshy and damp, and in the summer heat the soldiers and sailors became very ill with malaria. Food and water supplies ran out and many of them deserted. By September, the situation was desperate. Antony and Cleopatra decided that they must try to smash through the Roman blockade.

Helping hands

Antony and Cleopatra's army was made up of Roman and Egyptian soldiers, together with soldiers from many different lands. The kings of countries controlled by Antony such as Libya, Cilicia (part of modern Turkey), and Arabia sent soldiers to fight with Antony.

ADMIRAL AGRIPPA

Octavian's advisers included Marcus Vispanius Agrippa (64 BC–12 BC) one of Rome's most famous army commanders. Octavian knew that he could trust Agrippa, and that he understood naval strategy and tactics far better than Antony or Cleopatra.

Agrippa

Octavian

• Octavian's camp

SAILS READY!

Egyptian and Roman warships did not usually carry sails into battle, because they were heavy and took up valuable space. Instead, warships were powered by men rowing with oars. Before the Battle of Actium Antony and Cleopatra ordered their warships to have sails ready to hoist. They hoped to smash through the Roman blockade, and sail away as soon as they reached the open sea.

BATTLE TACTICS

Both sides made careful plans before fighting the Battle of Actium in September 31 BC. Octavian aimed to lure Antony and Cleopatra's ships out of the gulf, and then overpower them with his much larger fleet. Antony gave orders for his ships to fight their way through the middle of the Roman blockade.

FACT file

- When Antony and Cleopatra arrived in Greece at the beginning of the campaign they had about 300 Roman and 200 Egyptian warships. By the Battle of Actium they only had about 230 ships, and about 20,000 soldiers.
- Octavian had about 400 ships in his fleet and 37,000 soldiers.
- Cleopatra managed to escape with her own squadron of 60 ships, which included her treasure ship.

Gulf of Ambracia

• Actium

TRAPPED!
Cleopatra and Antony's warships were moored inside the Gulf of Ambracia, near Actium. The only way out of the gulf was to sail out into the Ionian sea.

• Antony's camp

IONIAN SEA

A LOSING BATTLE

The Romans and Egyptians fought battles at sea in two different ways. First, they tried ramming enemy warships with their ships' strong bronze "beaks" (sharp spikes, attached to the front of the ship). If this failed, they used ropes and hooks to snatch enemy ships and haul them alongside, so that the soldiers could jump from deck to deck and fight a battle with swords, as if they were on land.

CLEOPATRA SAILS AWAY

Once out in the open sea, Cleopatra realized she could escape. She took her chance, and sailed away. Her enemies said this was cowardly, but in fact, it was a wise decision, and may have been planned with Antony. She hoped to save her ships and her treasure so that she could fight another day. Antony managed to sail after Cleopatra, but the rest of his warships could not get past the Romans. His ships were destroyed, many of his soldiers were killed and most of them surrendered to Octavian.

Victorious return
After the Battle of Actium, Cleopatra sailed back into Alexandria harbour with flags flying as if she had won a great victory. She was afraid her enemies might not let her back into the city if they knew that she had been defeated by Octavian.

To the shores of the Red Sea
To protect her fleet from the Romans, Cleopatra ordered that her warships be hauled overland, from the Mediterranean to the Red Sea. But one of Cleopatra's neighbours and enemies, the King of Nabatea, set fire to the warships and destroyed them all.

STONE CARVING
Skilled stoneworkers would have worked on Cleopatra's tomb. They decorated the outside with beautiful designs, carved into the surface of the stone.

MAGNIFICENT MAUSOLEUM
Cleopatra knew that her future was uncertain if Octavian invaded Egypt. She began to experiment with poisons, and gave orders that work on her mausoleum (large tomb-chamber) was completed as soon as possible.

DEFEAT AND DISHONOUR

DEFEAT AT THE BATTLE OF ACTIUM plunged Antony into despair. He hid away on Pharos, an island in Alexandria harbour, and refused to see anyone. But Cleopatra bravely made plans to continue as Egypt's ruler. Her spies told her that Octavian did not have enough gold to pay his armies, so he could not attack immediately. But Cleopatra knew Octavian would attack sooner or later, because he needed Egypt's wealth. In time, Antony came out of hiding, and once again splendid banquets were held in the palace. Almost a year after Actium, the news came – the Romans were on their way. Cleopatra sent a message to Octavian, offering to give up her throne if he would let her children rule. But Octavian did not reply – it was clear that Octavian wanted to rule Egypt himself, for Rome. Antony rallied his army and rode out of the city to face Octavian.

GOLD AND JEWELS

As soon as her mausoleum was completed, Cleopatra gave orders for her treasures to be stored there. She believed that her spirit would survive after death to enjoy them. More importantly, she wanted to keep her gold and jewels safe. Cleopatra announced that she would set fire to the mausoleum and destroy the treasure if the Roman army marched on Alexandria.

Hellenistic (Greek) gold earrings

6 6 All swore to end their lives together, and until that time they charmed their days with a succession of glorious banquets. 9 9

Plutarch, from his
Life of Mark Antony
c. AD 75

EGYPT'S WEALTH
Octavian invaded Egypt because he needed gold. It is reported that he had all Cleopatra's treasure melted down, so that he could make coins to pay his armies.

Precious stones and metals such as turquoise and gold were mined in Egypt to make beautiful jewellery.

ROYAL TOMB
Cleopatra's mausoleum was probably built in the Ptolemies' royal cemetery, near the tomb of Alexander the Great. The mausoleum's remains are yet to be found.

A gold falcon, symbol of the Egyptian god Horus

Beautiful tombs were important to Greeks and Egyptians. They were houses in which they believed the dead person's spirit lived.

Dionysus, god of wine, song, and laughter

Dionysus holds a bunch of grapes, symbol of wine.

DIONYSUS
Antony believed that he was protected by the god Dionysus. Sometimes he felt he had become the god. The Greek historian Plutarch tells a chilling story: the night before Octavian marched on Alexandria, the citizens heard the sound of laughter and footsteps leaving the city. They said this showed that Dionysus had deserted Antony.

The death of Antony

ANTONY WAS FORCED to flee from Octavian's army when most of his soldiers refused to fight. Antony was disgraced and ashamed, and he blamed Cleopatra. Afraid of his anger, Cleopatra locked herself in her mausoleum and sent a message saying she was dead. In despair, Antony stabbed himself. When she heard the news, Cleopatra sent her servants to carry Antony to her, and he died in her arms.

THE DEATH OF CLEOPATRA

WITHIN WEEKS OF ANTONY'S SUICIDE in 30 BC, Cleopatra was dead, and Egypt was governed by Rome. Cleopatra was the last independent ruler of Egypt, and her death marked the end of over 3,000 glorious years of Egyptian civilization and Egyptian power. Although she did her best to defend her country, clever, charming Cleopatra could not defy the might of Rome. After Antony died, Roman troops surrounded Cleopatra's mausoleum, and kept her prisoner there. But Octavian treated her well. He allowed Cleopatra to arrange Antony's funeral, and to take part in the ceremony. But, he would not agree to let Cleopatra's children rule Egypt on behalf of Rome. So Cleopatra decided she must die. She could not bear to live while foreigners ruled her land. At her death, Egypt lost its most famous – and possibly its greatest – queen.

A FINAL FEAST

It is said that before her death Cleopatra ordered a splendid feast. She then asked one of her servants to smuggle in a poisonous snake in a basket of figs. After Cleopatra had eaten, she sent a note to Octavian asking to be buried with Antony. Alarmed, Octavian sent guards to find her, but it was too late. Cleopatra was already dead.

Carvings and columns
This funeral stele (carved upright stone) gives an idea of the style of buildings in the time of the Ptolemies. The doorway to Cleopatra's mausoleum may have looked like this.

> **"** Then somebody said in anger: "A fine deed, this, Charmion!" "It is indeed most fine," she said, "and befitting the descendant of so many kings." **"**
>
> Plutarch, from his
> *Life of Mark Antony*
> *c. AD 75*

Guardian goddesses
This painting on a sarcophagus (stone coffin) shows the goddess Isis and her sister Nephthys watching over a dead body. In Egyptian legends they brought the dead back to life.

A mysterious end

CLEOPATRA'S BODY HAS never been discovered, so historians do not know exactly how she died. There are stories that she experimented with poisons, and that she even tested some of them on slaves.

Bitten by an asp

The most popular story about Cleopatra's death says that she was bitten by a small poisonous snake, called an asp. But an asp would not have been able to bite Cleopatra and her two servants.

Figs, a sweet fruit, were a popular delicacy.

Death by asp bite is said to be quick and painless.

FAITHFUL SERVANTS
Cleopatra's faithful servants, Iras and Charmion, were found dead and dying beside her. They probably believed that they would go on serving her in the afterlife.

Charmion was the last to die.

Cleopatra let the snake bite her, and in seconds she was dead.

Cleopatra chose to be dressed like her favourite goddess Isis, who was honoured as the special protector of Egyptian pharoahs and queens.

Funeral ceremony

Cleopatra's mausoleum has not been found, so historians do not know whether her funeral followed Greek or Egyptian traditions. However, Cleopatra worshipped many Egyptian gods so it is probable that her funeral followed Egyptian traditions. It is likely to have been a simple ceremony because Octavian would have wanted the people of Egypt to forget their queen and accept him as their ruler.

A traditional
Egyptian funeral

AFTER CLEOPATRA

The death of Cleopatra made it easy for Octavian and the Roman army to complete their conquest of Egypt. In 30 BC, Octavian declared himself to be the new pharoah of Egypt. To show that they were now in control, Roman soldiers defaced ancient Egyptian monuments and destroyed official documents – including most of those created while Cleopatra was in power. For the next 500 years, Egypt became part of the Roman empire, ruled by governors appointed by Rome. Alexandria continued to be a great centre of learning and trade, but elsewhere Egypt's power and prosperity began to decline.

The Nile crocodile was an instantly recognizable symbol of Egypt.

Egypt captured
In 28 BC Roman leader Octavian issued this coin – the Latin words mean "Egypt captured" – to commemorate the death of Cleopatra and Antony and to celebrate Rome's conquest of Egypt.

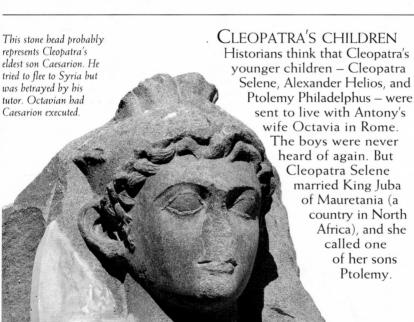

This stone head probably represents Cleopatra's eldest son Caesarion. He tried to flee to Syria but was betrayed by his tutor. Octavian had Caesarion executed.

CLEOPATRA'S CHILDREN
Historians think that Cleopatra's younger children – Cleopatra Selene, Alexander Helios, and Ptolemy Philadelphus – were sent to live with Antony's wife Octavia in Rome. The boys were never heard of again. But Cleopatra Selene married King Juba of Mauretania (a country in North Africa), and she called one of her sons Ptolemy.

HOMAGE TO A HERO
After Octavian had completed his conquest of Egypt, he went to visit the tomb of Alexander the Great in Alexandria. Cleopatra VII – and the Ptolemy dynasty (family) – were descended from one of Alexander the Great's generals. When Octavian was asked if he wanted to visit the tombs of the Ptolemies, he said he had come to honour a hero, not to see dead kings and queens.

ALEXANDER THE GREAT
(356–323 BC)

Cleopatra's place in history
Cleopatra's death marked the end of a glorious era in Egyptian history.

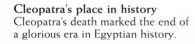

C. 2,500 BC THE PYRAMIDS
AT GIZA WERE BUILT

343–332 BC
PERSIAN KINGS
RULED EGYPT

323–30 BC
THE PTOLEMIES
RULED EGYPT

51–30 BC CLEOPATRA
VII (69–30 BC)
RULED EGYPT

| 500 BC | 400 BC | 300 BC | 200 BC | 100 BC | 0 |

C. 3,100–343 BC
EGYPTIAN PHAROAHS RULED EGYPT

332 BC
ALEXANDER THE GREAT
CONQUERED EGYPT

31 BC
BATTLE
OF ACTIUM

OCTAVIAN IN TRIUMPH

A year after Cleopatra died, Octavian staged a huge triumph (victory procession) to celebrate his conquest of Egypt. Antony and Cleopatra's children were probably made to march in the procession, alongside Cleopatra's fabulous treasures.

Gold and silver treasures were held high for all to see.

Weapons, armour, and other trophies were put on display.

Defeated rulers and their families were marched along in chains.

Laurel leaves
It was traditional for victorious Roman generals to be crowned with a laurel wreath.

Roman Egypt

AFTER EGYPT WAS conquered by Rome, it was known as the "Granary (grain-store) of the Roman empire". The empire needed huge amounts of wheat to feed Rome's vast army and the people who lived in the fast-growing cities, especially Rome. Other Egyptian products were popular in Rome, such as fine linens, papyrus, and perfumed oils. Egyptian scholars, poets, scientists, and gladiators were famous throughout the Roman world.

WHEAT

Fine papers
Papyrus (paper made from reeds grown in the Nile Delta) was exported to the lands of the Roman empire.

The Julian Calendar

In 46 BC, Roman leader Julius Caesar made changes to the Roman calendar, using scientific ideas first discovered by Greek and Egyptian astronomers, working together in Cleopatra's capital, Alexandria. Under the rule of the Ptolemies, the city became a great centre of learning, and visitors like Caesar carried Egyptian ideas and discoveries back to Rome. The calendar that is used in most countries today is based on these ideas.

This pocket sundial uses shadows cast by the string pointer to measure time. The astronomers of Ancient Egypt were the first to use the movements of the sun to measure time.

FORGOTTEN HERO?

Most of Mark Antony's statues were destroyed on Octavian's orders, but a wealthy Alexandrian paid to save Cleopatra's statues. Antony may have been forgotten in Egypt, but his image has survived on many Roman coins, and he was grandfather and great-grandfather to three Roman emperors – Caligula, Claudius, and Nero.

MARK ANTONY

AD 43 ROMANS INVADE AND CONQUER BRITAIN

AD 324 ROMAN EMPEROR CONSTANTINE DECLARES CHRISTIANITY THE OFFICIAL RELIGION OF THE ROMAN EMPIRE, INCLUDING EYGPT

C. 600–900 AD MUSLIM SOLDIERS AND SETTLERS FROM THE MIDDLE EAST BRING ISLAM TO EGYPT

| AD 100 | AD 200 | AD 300 | AD 400 | AD 500 | AD 600 |

27 BC–AD 14 OCTAVIAN (CAESAR AUGUSTUS) EMPEROR OF ROME

AD 395 ROMAN EMPIRE DIVIDED, WITH WESTERN EMPIRE BASED IN ROME AND EASTERN EMPIRE BASED IN CONSTANTINOPLE, TURKEY

AD 476 WESTERN ROMAN EMPIRE COMES TO AN END

CLEOPATRA'S STORY – FACT AND FICTION

Coins are often the only visual evidence that has survived.

Cleopatra VII is one of the most famous women who has ever lived. Her story has inspired poets, dramatists, and artists for over 2,000 years, and still fascinates us today. But, in fact, we know very little about her. The details of her life have been lost, or are shrouded in mystery. Only fragments of official documents dating from her reign have survived to tell us about her thoughts and deeds, and only a few carvings and sculptures remain to show us what she looked like. Most of our knowledge of Cleopatra comes from Greek and Roman writers who were loyal to Rome, and did not approve of her.

Queen Cleopatra
Some Ptolemaic queens, including Cleopatra VII, issued coins bearing their portraits. The coins are beautiful and were probably designed to create a good public image. This gold coin bears the portrait of another Ptolemaic queen – Cleopatra I.

Hieroglyphs
Cleopatra's name would have been carved or written, using Egyptian hieroglyphs (pictures and symbols), on temple walls and royal decrees.

A Greek name
Greek was the official language of Egypt in Cleopatra's time. So her name would also have been carved or written in Greek letters, as here.

Portrait of a queen
We can tell that this carving represents a Ptolemaic queen because it shows a royal crown and an elaborate Greek hairstyle, of corkscrew curls. It is a portrait of Cleopatra I or II.

WHICH CLEOPATRA?
Some sculptures inscribed (carved) with the name "Cleopatra" have survived. But there were at least seven queens named Cleopatra in the Ptolemaic dynasty (ruling family) and Cleopatra VII was the last.

ALEXANDRIA UNDER THE SEA
Alexandria is a big, modern city today, but the royal quarter where Cleopatra VII lived was flooded after an earthquake in the 14th century AD. In 1992, French archaeologist Franck Goddio and a team of divers started to explore the site. They have found a variety of statues and artefacts, and hope to find the lost palace of Cleopatra.

From hearsay to history

THE GREEK HISTORIAN, Plutarch (c. AD 50–120) described Cleopatra in his biography (life-story) of Mark Antony. Plutarch started to write his stories almost a hundred years after Cleopatra lived. He based his work on eyewitness accounts collected by his grandfather Lamprias, and on documents which no longer survive today. It is difficult to tell whether his stories about Cleopatra are true.

PLUTARCH

Parallel Lives
His *Life of Mark Antony* is one of a series of texts in which Plutarch compared Greek and Roman heroes.

ANTONY AND CLEOPATRA
Over 1,500 years after Plutarch died, English playwright William Shakespeare (1554–1616) was inspired by Plutarch's stories to write a play about Cleopatra and her love for Antony.

WILLIAM SHAKESPEARE

BEAUTIFUL FANTASY
Writers, artists, and, later, film-makers have been inspired by Cleopatra throughout history. Artist Sir Lawrence Alma-Tadema (1836–1912) painted imaginary scenes from Ancient Egypt and Rome. Here, he imagines Cleopatra as she waited for Antony in Tarsus.

CARRY ON CLEO
The legend of Cleopatra inspired comedy as well as tragedy. The 1965 comic film *Carry on Cleo*, portrayed Cleopatra as pretty and quite powerful, but not really suitable to be queen. Throughout history, people have often refused to take women rulers seriously.

PLAY FOR TODAY
William Shakespeare's play, *Antony and Cleopatra*, brilliantly brought the tragic love story of Cleopatra and Antony to life. Portraying a strong character like Cleopatra is a challenge relished by many actresses. In this scene from the play, staged in London in 1999, the role of Cleopatra is played by international star Helen Mirren.

HOLLYWOOD BLOCKBUSTER
In 1963, Hollywood film-makers completed a screen epic about Cleopatra and Antony. It starred a real-life couple, Elizabeth Taylor and Richard Burton, but it was not historically accurate. This scene from *Cleopatra* shows a lavish feast.

Index

Acknowledgments

The publisher would like to thank: Rachel Hilford, Sally Hamilton and Diane Legrande for picture research; Selina Wood for editorial help; David Gillingwater for early visuals; and Chris Bernstein for the index.

The publisher would like to thank the following for their kind permission to reproduce their photographs:

a=above; b=below; c=centre; l=left; r=right; t=top

AKG London: 19tr, 36-37; Cameraphoto, State Art Museum, Bucharest: *Cleopatra Dissolves the Pearl* Anton Schoonyans 33tr; Erich Lessing 40cl. **Ancient Art & Architecture Collection:** 27br, 45cb, 46tr; Dr. S. Coyne 9tl; G. T. Garvey 17cr; Ronald Sheridan 2cl, 8tl, 33cr, 41tl. **Dr Sally-Ann Ashton:** 15tr. **Bildarchiv Preußischer Kulturbesitz:** Antikenmuseum: Johannes Laurentius 13. **Bridgeman Art Library, London/New York:** Antony and Cleopatra Sir Lawrence Alma-Tadema 47tr; Louvre, France: Cleopatra Disembarking at Tarsus Claude Lorrain 30tl. **British Museum, London:** 19cr, 20cla, 20cl, 20t, 21tc, 25tr, 26bl, 33br, 35cra, 35crb, 37tl, 41cr, 45cbl. **Mary Evans Picture Library:** 6-7, 25b, 43br, 47tl. **Werner Forman Archive:** British Museum 44tr; Private Collection 21tr. **Ronald Grant Archive:** Carry on Cleo 1963 © EMI/Peter Roger's Production 47cr; Cleopatra 1963 © Twentieth Century Fox 24tr, 47bl. **Performing Arts Library:** Fritz Curzon 47br. **Popperfoto:** 46br. **Scala Group S.p.A.:** Arte romana Vaticano Cortile delle Corazze 0tl; Vaticano Museo Gregoriano Egizio 41cla. **Science Museum:** 14br, 45cr.

Jacket: **Ancient Art & Architecture Collection:** front cl. **Bildarchiv Preußischer Kulturbesitz, Berlin 2000:** Antikenmuseum: Johannes Laurentius front cll. **Scala Group S.p.A.:** Vaticano Museo Gregoriano Egizio back cr.